Christmas with the PROPHETS

Compiled by
LAURA F. WILLES

DESERET
BOOK

Salt Lake City, Utah

ISBN 978-1-60907-142-4

Printed in the United States of America
Artistic Printing, Salt Lake City, Utah

10   9   8   7   6   5   4   3   2   1

A Message from

JOSEPH SMITH

"And we beheld the glory of the Son, on the right hand of the Father, and received of his fulness; and saw the holy angels, and them who are sanctified before his throne, worshiping God, and the Lamb, who worship him forever and ever.

"And now, after the many testimonies which have been given of him, this is the testimony, last of all, which we give of him: That he lives! For we saw him, even on the right hand of God; and we heard the voice bearing record that he is the Only Begotten of the Father—that by him, and through him, and of him, the worlds are and were created, and the inhabitants thereof are begotten sons and daughters unto God" (D&C 76:20–24).

A Message from

BRIGHAM YOUNG

"Where are the individuals that can say that they *know* that Jesus lives? And who are the individuals that can say that his gospel is true and is the plan of salvation to man? . . . To me it is

certain, that *no man lives on the face of the earth, no woman lives, that can say this, except those to whom Christ has revealed himself.*

" . . . There is one class of people, and one only, that live upon the face of the earth, who do know it; and that class of men and women are *those that keep his commandments and do his will;* none others can say it. None others can declare with boldness, and emphatically, that Jesus lives and that his gospel is true."[1]

A Message from JOHN TAYLOR

"The coming of the Savior to the world, his suffering, death, resurrection and ascension to the position he occupies in the eternal world before his Heavenly Father, has a great deal to do with our interests and happiness; . . . he came . . . to secure the salvation and exaltation of the human family."[2] "And I say, O Lord, hasten the day! Let Zion be established! Let the mountain of the Lord's house be established on the tops of the mountains!"[3]

A Message from WILFORD WOODRUFF

"There is no being that has power to save the souls of men and give them eternal life, except the Lord Jesus Christ, under the command of His Father.

"It should be our chief study to treasure up the words of life that we may grow in grace and advance in the knowledge

of God and become perfected in Christ Jesus, that we may receive a fullness and become heirs of God and joint heirs of Jesus Christ."[4]

"...While we travel through this world of change and sorrow, may we take pattern by the lives of the worthy . . . and . . . follow in the steps of the great Exemplar of all righteousness, our Lord Jesus Christ, whose grace be ever with you all."[5]

A Message from LORENZO SNOW

"When Jesus lay in the manger, a helpless infant, He knew not that He was the Son of God, and that formerly He created the earth. When the edict of Herod was issued, He knew nothing of it; He had not power to save Himself; and His father and mother had to take Him and fly into Egypt to preserve Him from the effects of that edict. Well, He grew up to manhood, and during His progress it was revealed unto Him who He was, and for what purpose He was in the world. The glory and power He possessed before He came into the world was made known unto Him. It was not a very pleasurable thing to be placed upon the cross and to suffer the excruciating torture that He bore for hours, in order to accomplish the work for which He had come upon the earth, . . . [yet He suffered it] for the salvation of the world."[6]

A Message from

JOSEPH F. SMITH

"The knowledge that God is with us, and that his work will prevail, should buoy us up under every difficulty and every trial, having the conviction that the Lord will cause even 'the wrath of man to praise him.' The very efforts of the enemies of his Church to hedge up its way will be overruled by him to accelerate its advancement. . . .

" . . . Bless the children; provide for the poor; comfort the distressed; visit the widow and the fatherless; forgive those who may be regarded as enemies; be filled with the spirit of blessing; have charity for all; promote peace and good will, and spread abroad the light and intelligence which flow down from heaven in the gospel of the Son of God; recognize his divine hand in all that is good and useful and that promotes the welfare of humanity. . . . Let all nations join in the glad refrain which was sung by the angels at the Savior's birth.

" . . . We extend greeting and blessing and earnest desire for the favor of heaven to rest upon all the human family, with the fervent hope that the time is not far distant when they will bow the knee to King Immanuel and sing with united voice, Glory to God and the Lamb for ever and ever."[7]

A Message from
HEBER J. GRANT

"Let Christmas . . . be celebrated everywhere. Let the little ones be made glad. Let peace and love, benevolence and charity abound. Let forgiveness and patience and tolerance drive out all animosities, and let us all serve God and help our neighbor, and put on Christ and follow Him, as well as celebrate His birth on earth."[8]

"Our celebration of the Christmastide should be so ordered that holy angels can approve and in spirit participate with us. . . . May families be united and individuals moved upon by the Christmas Spirit in rich measure, that thanksgiving and praise, accompanied by benevolent ministry to those in need, may sanctify our hearts and homes!"[9]

"To members of the Church throughout the world, and to peace-lovers everywhere, we say, behold in this Man of Galilee not merely a great Teacher, not merely a peerless Leader, but the Prince of Peace, the Author of Salvation, here and now, literally and truly the Savior of the World!"[10]

A Message from
GEORGE ALBERT SMITH

"The promises of the Lord can be relied upon in the future as they have been in the past. Each passing year brings us nearer the date of his coming in power and glory. True, the hour and the day, no man knoweth. But the duty of the Latter-day Saints is

to watch and pray, being valiant for the truth and abounding in good works. Despite the discontent in the world and the apparent growth of the power of evil, those who continue to stand in holy places can discern through it all the handiwork of the Lord in the consummation of his own purposes. The Almighty reigns and will continue to reign!

"Therefore, at this season of the year, let personal discords be forgotten and animosities banished. Let rejoicing be heartfelt but not boisterous. Let gift giving be as generous as circumstances will allow, but not extravagant. Let the hearts of the children be made glad, and let us live that the spirit of the Prince of Peace may dwell in our homes."[11]

A Message from
DAVID O. MCKAY

"The spirit of the world is antagonistic to the establishment of peace or freedom—and these can come only through compliance with the ethical and spiritual and eternal principles proclaimed and lived by Jesus of Nazareth, the crucified Christ, the risen Lord, the Prince of Peace.

"This Christmas Eve as darkness envelops the earth, each of you will retire with absolute confidence that the night will pass and that on Christmas morning the earth will be filled again with the light of day. Of this we have not a shadow of doubt.

"As absolute as the certainty we have in our hearts that to-night will be followed by dawn tomorrow morning so is my assurance that Jesus Christ is the Savior of mankind, the light that

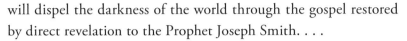

will dispel the darkness of the world through the gospel restored by direct revelation to the Prophet Joseph Smith. . . .

> *"O Living Christ who still*
> *Dost all our burdens share,*
> *Come now and dwell within the hearts*
> *Of all men everywhere."* [12]

A Message from
JOSEPH FIELDING SMITH

"I greet you at this Christmas season, in love and fellowship, and with prayer that our Eternal Father will look down upon you in mercy and pour out His bounteous blessings upon you. . . .

"We need to know that in spite of all the troubles and ills which befall us, still the Lord is governing in the affairs of the earth and that if we keep His commandments and are true and faithful to His laws, He will bless us here and now and reward us with eternal life in His kingdom in due course. . . .

" . . . I . . . now pray at this Christmas Season, and at all times, we may center our faith in the Son of God and gain for ourselves the peace which passeth understanding." [13]

A Message from
HAROLD B. LEE

"This traditional season for celebrating the birth of Jesus Christ is an occasion for rejoicing and for worshipping the Eternal

God whose greatest gift to mankind was His Beloved Son. This . . . should be a season in which we turn from all worldly cares and from selfishness and despair in order to seek heavenly gifts of eternal value. . . .

"The Master's teachings constantly emphasized . . . love, tolerance, compassion, honesty, kindness and humility. He was the great peacemaker. . . . He further taught us how to overcome the evils of ignorance, hate, lust, falsity, revenge, fear, and contempt by learning and doing the will of the Father. . . .

"These sacred principles were His formula for success, which when lived, brings peace and happiness in this life and exaltation hereafter."[14]

A Message from
SPENCER W. KIMBALL

"Though we make an effort to follow the [Savior's] pattern of gift giving, sometimes our program becomes an exchange—gift given for gift expected. Never did the Savior give in expectation. I know of no case in his life in which there was an exchange. He was always the giver, seldom the recipient. Never did he give shoes, hose, or a vehicle; never did he give perfume, a shirt, or a fur wrap. His gifts were of such a nature that the recipient could hardly exchange or return the value. His gifts were rare ones: eyes to the blind, ears to the deaf, and legs to the lame; cleanliness to the unclean, wholeness to the infirm, and breath to the lifeless. His gifts were opportunity to the downtrodden, freedom to the oppressed, light in the darkness, forgiveness to the repentant, hope to the despairing. His friends gave him shelter, food, and

love. He gave them of himself, his love, his service, his life. The wise men brought him gold and frankincense. He gave them and all their fellow mortals resurrection, salvation, and eternal life. We should strive to give as he gave. To give of oneself is a holy gift. . . .

"He whose birthday we celebrate is the Son of God, the Eternal Father. In him is all majesty and power. No life is comparable to his. He stands alone on the pinnacle of all that is holy and good and righteous and exemplary. My heart is filled with joy to know that he marked for us the plan, the way of life, whereby if we are faithful we may someday see him and express our gratitude personally for his perfect life and his sacrifice for us. . . .

" . . . We can do nothing more to show our love for him than to give of ourselves in a silent, quiet, loving way. This, the gift of self, is the highest gift of all."[15]

A Message from
EZRA TAFT BENSON

"The real purpose of Christmas is to worship Him whose birth is commemorated during this season. How might we do that? By giving. Certainly there are genuine feelings of love and friendship wrapped up in the beautiful packages we exchange with those dear to us. But I'm concerned about another kind of giving. Considering all that the Savior has given and continues to give us, is there something we might give Him in return this Christmastime?

"Christ's great gift to us was His life and sacrifice. Should that not then be our small gift to Him—our lives and sacrifices . . . ?

"[Christmas] prompts us to be more tolerant and giving, more conscious of others, more generous and genuine, more filled with hope and charity and love—all Christlike attributes. No wonder the spirit of Christmas touches the hearts of people the world over. Because for at least a time, increased attention and devotion are turned toward our Lord and Savior, Jesus Christ. . . .

"Not many years hence Christ will come again. He will come in power and might as King of kings and Lord of lords. And ultimately every knee will bow and every tongue confess that Jesus is the Christ.

"But I testify *now* that Jesus is the Christ and that He *lives*."[16]

A Message from
HOWARD W. HUNTER

"The real Christmas comes to him who has taken Christ into his life as a moving, dynamic, vitalizing force. The real spirit of Christmas lies in the life and mission of the Master. . . .

"If you desire to find the true spirit of Christmas and partake of the sweetness of it, let me make this suggestion to you. During the hurry of the festive occasion of this Christmas season, find time to turn your heart to God. Perhaps in the quiet hours, and in a quiet place, and on your knees—alone or with loved ones—give thanks for the good things that have come to you, and ask that his spirit might dwell in you as you earnestly strive to serve him and keep his commandments. He will take you by the hand and his promises will be kept."[17]

"If our lives and our faith are centered on Jesus Christ and his restored gospel, nothing can ever go permanently wrong. On the other hand, if our lives are not centered on the Savior and his teachings, no other success can ever be permanently right."[18]

A Message from
GORDON B. HINCKLEY

"His Only Begotten Son [came] into the world to bring hope into our hearts, to bring kindness and courtesy into our relationships, and above all to save us from our sins and guide us on the way that leads to eternal life. . . .

"This is the wondrous and true story of Christmas. The birth of Jesus in Bethlehem of Judea is preface. The three-year ministry of the Master is prologue. The magnificent substance of the story is His sacrifice, the totally selfless act of dying in pain on the cross of Calvary to atone for the sins of all of us.

"The epilogue is the miracle of the Resurrection, bringing the assurance that 'as in Adam all die, even so in Christ shall all be made alive' (1 Cor. 15:22). . . .

"For each of you may this be a merry Christmas. But more importantly, I wish for each of you a time, perhaps only an hour, spent in silent meditation and quiet reflection on the wonder and the majesty of this, the Son of God. Our joy at this season is because He came into the world. The peace that comes from Him, His infinite love which each of us may feel, and an overwhelming sense of gratitude for that which He freely gave us at so great a cost to Himself—these are of the true essence of Christmas."[19]

A Message from

THOMAS S. MONSON

"Then came that night of nights when the angel of the Lord came upon shepherds abiding in the field, keeping watch over their flock, and the pronouncement, 'For unto you is born this day in the city of David a Saviour, which is Christ the Lord.' (Luke 2:11.)

"Thus, personally invited to undertake a search for the babe wrapped in swaddling clothes and lying in a manger, did these shepherds concern themselves with the security of their possessions? Did they procrastinate their search for Jesus? The record affirms that the shepherds said to one another, 'Let us now go even unto Bethlehem. . . . And they came with haste.' (Luke 2:15–16.) . . .

"Before we can successfully undertake a personal search for Jesus, we must first prepare time for him in our lives and room for him in our hearts. In these busy days there are many who have time for golf, time for shopping, time for work, time for play—but no time for Christ. . . .

" . . . This is the Jesus whom we seek. This is our brother whom we love. This is Christ the Lord, whom we serve. I testify that he lives, for I speak as one who has found him."[20]

ENDNOTES

1. Brigham Young, in Joseph Fielding McConkie, *Journal of Discourses Digest* (Salt Lake City: Bookcraft, 1975), 52–53; emphasis in original.

2. John Taylor, in *Journal of Discourses, 26 vols.* (Liverpool: Latter-day Saints' Book Depot, 1854–86), 10:115.

3. John Taylor, in Truman Madsen, *The Presidents of the Church: Insights into Their Lives and Teachings* (Salt Lake City: Deseret Book, 2004), 69.

4. Wilford Woodruff, *Teachings of Presidents of the Church: Wilford Woodruff* (Salt Lake City: The Church of Jesus Christ of Latter-day Saints, 2004), 74.

5. Wilford Woodruff, in The Latter-Day Saints' *Millennial Star* (July 9, 1888): 436–37.

6. Lorenzo Snow, in Conference Report, April 1901, 3.

7. "Greetings from the First Presidency," *Improvement Era* (January 1906): 247–48.

8. Heber J. Grant, in James R. Clark, comp. *Messages of the First Presidency of The Church of Jesus Christ of Latter-day Saints,* 6 vols. (Salt Lake City: Bookcraft, 1965–75), 5:167.

9. Ibid., 5:287.

10. Ibid., 6:39.

11. George Albert Smith, "To the Latter-day Saints Everywhere," *Improvement Era* (December 1947): 797.

12. David O. McKay, "This Christmastide," *Improvement Era* (December 1951), 861, 938; poem by John Oxenham, 1852–1941.

13. Joseph Fielding Smith, "Christmas Greetings from President Joseph Fielding Smith to the Members of the Church throughout the World," *Church News,* December 19, 1970, 3.

14. Harold B. Lee, N. Eldon Tanner, and Marion G. Romney, "A Christmas Message," *Church News,* December 22, 1973, 8–9.

15. Spencer W. Kimball, *The Wondrous Gift* (Salt Lake City: Deseret Book, 1978), 1–2, 6–7.

16. Ezra Taft Benson, *President Ezra Taft Benson Remembers the Joys of Christmas* (Salt Lake City: Deseret Book, 1988), 10–13; emphasis in original.

17. Howard W. Hunter, "The Real Christmas," in *Speeches of the Year, 1972–73* (Provo, Utah: Brigham Young University Press, 1973), 68–69.

18. Howard W. Hunter, in Clyde J. Williams, ed. *The Teachings of Howard W. Hunter* (Salt Lake City: Bookcraft, 1997), 40.

19. Gordon B. Hinckley, "The Wondrous and True Story of Christmas," *Ensign,* December 2000, 3–5.

20. Thomas S. Monson, "The Search for Jesus," *Ensign,* December 1990, 2, 4, 5.